The Last Time I Saw My Dad

A short story by Richard Greene

The cover picture of my father was taken in 1950. The picture is of poor quality, and sadly, it is one of only a very few photographs I have of my father.

About the Author

Richard and his Lhasa Apso Jackson

About the Author

Please visit my web page, www.richardjgreene.net, or visit me on Facebook at https://www.facebook.com/richardgreene.7393 or on

Twitter at https://twitter.com/@dickiejoe All of my books are available on Amazon as ebook or paperback.

The Last Time I Saw My Dad

Contents

One

The year was 1961; it was July, I had been out of the Navy for over a year and was considering where I should go on my first vacation from Burlington Truck Lines, where I worked in the office. Thinking I had not been down to Houston, Texas, to see my Dad in a while, I boarded a Greyhound Bus in Denver and took the long trip. A day and a half later, as I stepped from the bus into the hot, humid afternoon, I was met by someone that barely resembled the man I last saw in the early summer of 1956. He was heavier, his face plump, and his once thick, black hair thinner and filled with gray. He smiled, looking glad to see me, and as I got off the bus, we shook hands. (Men did not hug in those days) Carrying my small bag of belongings, I walked with him to the parking lot where his blue 1953 four-door Mercury awaited; the same car I had driven the last time I visited back in 1956.

It was a long, warm ride in a car without air conditioning from the bus terminal in downtown Houston to the west side and Washington Avenue, where he lived. The warm Texas breeze passing through the car's open windows played with my hair and the collar of my shirt as we talked. He asked about Mom, how things were around the house, my grandparents, and finally, my brothers, Ed, Jerry, and Malcolm. He specifically asked how my brother Jerry was.

Mentioning Jerry took me back to the night, Dad walked out of the house in Englewood, Colorado, a small suburb of Denver, never to return. He came home drunk in the early morning hours, as he often had, and went into my older brother Jerry's bedroom, where he and his wife Sylvia lay sleeping. For reasons known only to my Dad, he slapped my bother out of a sound sleep. Jerry, who was no longer a young boy but a good-sized man himself, jumped out of bed wearing only his underwear, and the two fought.

Waking from a sound sleep on the cot in a small room off of the kitchen by the commotion, I rushed through the kitchen into the living room, where I stood at the bedroom door, finding a terrible scene. Sylvia was standing in the far corner in her nightgown, looking terrified, while my mother cried and pleaded for my Dad and brother to stop fighting. I stood at the open doorway watching with wide eyes as Dad and Jerry cursed one another, rolling off of the bed onto the floor next to my dog. Shep was a good size Collie, German Sheppard mix that quickly crawled under the bed to get out of the way. Jerry somehow managed to get Dad in a headlock, holding him down on the floor. After several minutes of squirming, Dad settled down, stopped moving, then asked Jerry not to hit him anymore. My brother asked him if he'd had enough, Dad said yes, so Jerry slowly let go of the headlock and stood. As he stepped back toward the bedroom window, he looked down at Dad and said, "You've hit me for the last time, you son of a bitch."

Dad rolled over, sat up on the floor, his face bloody as he slowly stood with the help of the bed. My mother had hurried into the kitchen returning with two small towels handing one to each. Dad wiped the blood from his face and hands and then, without looking at anyone, walked past me, set the towel and the keys to the house and car on the coffee table, then walked out the front door. Scared and feeling sorry for him, I rushed to the bay window in the living room, pushed the drapes apart, and watched as he walked through the streetlamp's light on the corner, disappearing into the darkness. Mom was at my side with tears in her eyes, and as we both stared out the window into the darkness, she told me to go back to bed.

On my way back to the small room off of the kitchen and my cot, I paused at my brother's bedroom door. He sat on the edge of the bed, his head buried in his hands with Sylvia sitting beside him, crying. She looked up at me, smiled, and softly told me to go to bed. Feeling sorry for them both, I called my dog Shep and waited while he made his way from under the bed. Then he and I returned to the small room and my cot. Shep jumped up onto the foot of the bed and lay down, looking at me with his big, dark, sad eyes. Getting into bed, I called to him, and after he made the short trip and lay down next to me, I put my arms around him and began to cry.

Opening my eyes early the next morning, I wondered if what happened the night was but a dream. As sleepiness left me, I knew it had not been a dream. I got up and crept through the house past my brother's closed bedroom door to the open door of my parent's bedroom, where I peered inside to see if Dad had returned. Seeing only my mother's black hair sticking out from under the covers, I returned to my room, got dressed, then quietly made my way through the house to the front door. Stepping outside onto the front porch, I waited for Shep, then slowly and quietly, I closed the door, then the screen door. Sitting on the steps of the porch in the warm, early morning sun with Shep at my side, I waited for Dad.

While I stared at the empty street and waited, he boarded a Greyhound bus for Houston, Texas. That was in the early spring of 1952, and I was twelve years of age.

Two

When Dad arrived in Houston, he lived with his brother Henry while he looked for work as a Carpenter, which was his trade, and he was good at it. The days passed, and one afternoon, a woman named Mary Laborde, who owned the house next door to Uncle Henry and his family, stopped by for a visit. She would occasionally do this while making her rounds to the other houses she owned.

Mary Laborde was a woman of some wealth, owning over fifty homes in the Houston area, all painted the same white with green trim. She also owned an exterminating business that took care of several of downtown Houston's large hotels and restaurants. She and her two daughters lived in a sprawling u-shaped ranch-style brick house with four bedrooms and three baths. The house, located on Memorial Drive, sat on two acres of lush green grass and shrubbery maintained by a gardener. When I first met the two girls, Elizabeth was twenty, thin and tall with long, light brown hair and blue eyes. Her younger sister, Evelyn, was eighteen, five-two, curvy, with big brown eyes and long, dark brown hair.

A few of Mary's visits passed, and one day, Dad got up the courage to ask her out to dinner and a movie. She accepted, and that began their relationship. Mary was thin but not skinny, with a fair complexion, and always wore her waist-long black and gray hair in a braid atop of her head. She was a simple dresser wearing house dresses that buttoned down the front and flat shoes. At some point, and why I never was told, Evelyn had a nervous breakdown and was hospitalized for a period. Dad would visit her almost daily, and at times, she would talk to him when she wouldn't talk to anyone else. Through this ordeal, they became quite close, and she began calling him Uncle Ed. Dad later told me that Evelyn was never quite the same after that.

Time passed, and Dad somehow convinced Mary to finance the building of a bar and a small four-room house behind it on a vacant lot he knew of on Washington Ave. Washington Ave was a rough and sometimes dangerous part of Houston, where almost every other building was a bar. They named the bar, The Lone Texan. I am not sure what the arrangements were, and I never asked, but I always suspected it was gratitude for the kindness he showed to her daughter Evelyn. Mary Laborde was very protective of her two girls, having lost an older daughter to Cancer. Something she never quite got over.

I was thirteen when I took my first trip to Houston on a Greyhound bus to visit Dad, and during that first summer and all summers after that, I would spend part of my time at Mary's house. I would listen to Evelyn practice the piano, or she and I would take walks in the wooded area behind the house and talk. Often we were accompanied by their five dogs, giving them a little time to run and play away from their kennel behind the small six-room guest house atop a four-car garage. I often played board games with the two girls, or Evelyn and I would go to an afternoon or evening movie that the Catholic Church Magazine approved. It seemed foolish to me not being a Catholic because we could not see what I thought were better movies. Evelyn was five years older than I, and when I would leave their house to return to the Lone Texan, she would hug me, kiss me on the cheek, smile, and say, "See you tomorrow, cousin." And I must admit, I looked forward to that hug and kiss on the cheek, and when I got older, the holding of hands in the darkness of a movie theater, her head resting on my shoulder.

Mary's ex-husband, Cleveland Laborde, was a Cajun from Louisiana with a thick Cajun accent. I had never heard that accent before, and it fascinated me. He lived in New Orleans most of the time but would visit his daughters now and again. After a few days, he would disappear for a couple of months, searching for buried pirate treasure somewhere in the Caribbean with two of his associates. I often wondered if he ever found anything of value. All of this I learned during my first visit to Houston.

Getting back to my visit, the Mercury turned off of Washington Avenue into the empty, familiar parking lot of The Lone Texan Bar that once was filled with cars belonging to customers. The single-story building of white wood siding, two bay windows separated by a double, wood-framed glass door seemed smaller than I remembered. (It seems that time has a way of making things smaller than we remember them.) Dad drove past the oak tree standing tall next to the building and stopped in its shade at the gate of the seven-foot-tall chain-link fence with barbed wire on the top. The fence ran from the bar's back corner around a tiny four-room house and small grassed yard to the other rear corner of the bar.

As I got out of the car, I glanced around the empty lot in memory. As my eyes settled on a side street, I recalled my first or second visit to Houston when Dad said he had some work to do on a house a few blocks away and wanted me to go with him. I recalled climbing into the back of his pickup and standing behind the cab, feeling the warm Texas air rush past me as he drove away from the bar. A few minutes later, the pickup stopped next to the curb at the end of the dead-end street. I jumped down and waited as Dad opened his door and climbed out. Curious where we were, I followed him up a narrow sidewalk covered in the shade of big trees toward a large, covered porch and front door of a white, two-story house with black trim.

A thin Negro lady appeared at the open door, paused a moment, then stepped through the screen door as we walked up the porch's steps. Letting the screen door slam, she smiled. "Good morning Mister Ed," she said, then looking at me, asked, "Who is this fine-looking boy y'all have with ya, Mr. Ed?"

Dad introduced me, and as I shook her hand, I noticed several scantily dressed Negro girls sitting in the parlor. I may not have been worldly, but I quickly figured out where we were. The lady smiled and asked if we would like to come inside for a visit and a glass of lemonade. Dad put his hand on my shoulder and said we sure would. I can still feel the warmth of my face as it flushed, and all I remember is the laughter that followed me as I headed back to the pickup truck and Dad asking where I was going.

The sound of the chain as Dad pulled it from around the gate and post brought me back to the present. Dad lifted the latch, pushed the gate open, stepped inside, and waited. After I was in the yard, he locked the gate, and then I followed him along a narrow sidewalk to the bar's back door. There we turned onto another sidewalk that cut a path through a small lawn in need of mowing to the door of the small house. He unlocked the door, and as I stepped inside, greeted by familiar odors I had long ago forgotten, it was as if I stepped back into 1956.

While Dad telephoned Mary to tell her we were back from the bus depot, I walked into the small second bedroom and tossed my bag on the bed that I slept on during my past visits. As I looked out the window at the rear door of the bar, memories raced through my mind of hot summer nights when I lay on top of the sheets next to the open window wearing only my underwear. As the air from the fan, cooled my skin, I would listen to the laughter and music spilling out the open rear door through the screen door of the bar, imagining what was going on inside. From memory, I could still smell the salt air from the Gulf of Mexico that sometimes made its way to Houston late at night. I was surprised at seeing two dusty, wooden model airplanes I had built and painted years ago still hanging from the ceiling with thumbtacks and black thread just as I had left them.

Dad hung up the telephone and asked if I wanted a soda or beer. Taking my eyes from the two model airplanes and the memories they brought back, I walked into the other room and said a beer sounded good. With our beers in hand, we stepped outside and sat down in two of the four white, weathered, wooden lawn chairs covered in shade and talked while waiting for Mary and the girls.

Three

Mary and her daughters Elizabeth and Evelyn stopped by later that afternoon to visit. Elizabeth had married a nice young man named Jack Fulbright, whom I had met during one of my previous visits. She seemed very happy.

Evelyn was Evelyn, and she was still a little silly at twenty-six. As she climbed out of the back seat of the black Lincoln, she yelled, "Cousin Richard." Hurrying through the fence gate, she ran across the yard and hugged me while kissing me on the cheek. Smiling, she wiped the red lipstick off with her finger. "You've grown up," she said, then asked how I have been.

"Doing okay," I told her. Then after a warm hello and a hug from Mary, Elizabeth shook my hand while saying it was good to see me and asked how the trip was. I told her it was long.

During the next few days, Mary and the girls would take Dad and me out to lunch or the house for a nice sit-down meal prepared by her Negro maid, who I remembered from before. Dad and I spent the days playing dominoes or sat outside in the weathered, white lawn chairs on the grass I had mowed with his old push mower. Though it all seemed the same, it was different somehow, and I thought of Thomas Wolf's 'You can't go home again.' we drank our beer and visited, and after a few moments, I asked why he closed the bar. He shrugged, saying it had become too much trouble and he was losing money.

The days quickly passed, and the day my bus was to leave for Denver, Dad and I spent the morning playing dominoes. We finished our fourth or fifth game when I became stiff from sitting. Picking up the beer I had been nursing, I stood, leaned against the jamb of the open door, and looked out the screen door. Turning, I watched Dad put the dominoes back in the box, then place the box on a shelf above the TV. Turning my attention to the locked gate of the chain-link fence, I thought it was already a hot, muggy morning.

Then I thought about the long bus ride home, knowing it would be stopping at every small town between

Houston and Denver. As my eyes settled on Dad's car, I thought about a young, slender Cajun girl named Ellen, with short, black hair, dark eyes, full lips, and olive skin, that used to live down the street from the bar.

My memory found the day I got out of the Mercury after returning from Mary's. Closing the car door, I saw this lovely young girl walking past the driveway to the parking lot. She smiled, and as I called out, she stopped, and we talked for a few minutes. We dated for a while that last summer of 1956 before I returned to Englewood, where I joined the Navy. Hot summer nights at the Hempstead Drive-In Theater north of Houston came to me, and then parking in front of her house while I worried her father would come out of the front door.

As I sipped my beer, I thought about the last time I saw her. It was my last night in Houston, and she had come to the fence where she stood in the light of the floodlight attached to the corner of the bar and called my name in a loud whisper. I remembered stepping outside the gate, taking her hand as we walked toward her house away from the floodlights. The music from the jukebox inside the bar slowly faded, leaving the sound of crickets and our footsteps on the gravel road to fill the warm night air.

We stood on the porch of her house under the soft, yellow porch light, and as tears rolled down her cheeks, she handed me a small, folded piece of paper that contained her name and address, asking me to write. I took the paper, shoved it into the pocket of my shirt, and said I would. Somehow I lost the piece of paper and never wrote.

Wondering what became of her, I turned to Dad and asked. He thought and said that he hadn't seen her in several years but seemed to recall hearing she married and moved to Dallas. Hoping she found happiness, I asked if her parents still lived down the street. Shaking his head, he said they had moved to Fort Worth last year or the year before. He wasn't sure which.

Memories of a young Russian immigrant named Dimitri and his four brothers living in the next block in one of Mary Laborde's houses crept into my mind. It was my second summer in Houston, and although Dimitri was a little older than I, Dad had asked if he would spend some time with me since I had no friends in Houston. Sometimes he and I would take the bus across town to the Shamrock Hotel, change into bathing suits in the bathroom of the lobby and spend the afternoon in the pool swimming as if we were guests. Dimitri was always chasing the girls, and in his thick Russian accent, he would grin and say he liked American girls. He loved to Polka, so on Friday nights, we would ride the bus to one of several open-air dances with live bands where I learned to Polka. I asked Dad if Dimitri and his brothers were still around, but Dad said the oldest had returned to Russia while Dimitri and the others moved to Corpus Christi a few years ago to work on the oil rigs.

I looked from the chain-link fence and the old Mercury to the locked back door of the bar. Recalling memories of what went on inside, I asked where the key was. Dad handed me a ring of keys holding up the one that unlocked the back door. Seeing he was curious, I set my empty bottle down, took the keys without explanation, and stepped outside. As the screen door slammed behind me, I walked the twenty yards to the back door of the bar, opened the screen door, and as it rested against my butt, I shoved the key into the lock and turned it. Pushing the door open, I stepped into the dead silence of the kitchen, greeted by musty smells, warm air, and dim light.

Leaving the keys in the lock and the door open, I walked through the narrow, dim kitchen past the black, flat top gas stove. I Remembered cooking hamburgers that I would eat in the house while drinking a beer I managed to steal from the cooler. I continued my journey, stopping in the doorway to the dimly lit bar where I spent much of my time as a young boy during those hot summers sitting under the now silent, still ceiling fans. A small amount of sunlight managed to get past the closed shutters of the two bay windows giving the room a ghostly appearance. As I stood bathed in silence, I imagined the people I had come to know in this place as they drank, laughed, and sometimes awkwardly danced the two-step to the music from the jukebox.

The long, red Formica bar covered with thick dust was off to my left. I could see the three small narrow wooden boxes affixed neatly under it at various places where Dad once kept his forty-five Semi-automatic pistols. The small bat with a leather strap through its handle hung on the wall behind the bar just above the empty cash register, a reminder of the kind of people that patronized The Lone Texan in those days. I walked past the chrome barstools with red, vinyl stuffed seats pushed neatly under the bar to the dusty, silent jukebox in the center of the room. Standing like a monument of the days long past, it pleased me to see it still contained the forty-five rpm records from another era. Five booths with green upholstery and red Formica tabletops lined both outer walls, and several small tables and chairs were scattered on both sides of the small area used for dancing.

A bowling shuffleboard machine sat in the right corner next to one of the shuttered windows that overlooked the parking lot leading to Washington Avenue. Fine sawdust mixed with dust-covered the narrow, wooden alley where a single puck sat idle, waiting for someone to drop a coin in the slot and slide it down the alley. On the other side of the room, past the wooden, framed glass door next to the other shuttered bay window, was a small table and four chairs neatly shoved under it. I imagined myself sitting at that table as I often had with my drawing paper, a bottle of India ink and pen drawing, or writing short stories in a notebook that had become casualties of time.

Walking up to the bar, I pulled the stool away from where I would sit and drink a soda while listening to music from the jukebox. Like a voyeur, I would sit in silence and watch the people. Dusting the stool off, I sat down, recalling the sounds of Johnny Cash singing Folsom Prison mix with the laughter, loud voices, and the bells of the shuffleboard as the puck slid under the pins. As I sat there glancing around the room, memories of the summers I spent here as a young boy raced through my mind like a movie. The Saturday afternoon when a slim, young, good-looking, blonde prostitute named Paula was standing at the jukebox dressed in a white blouse and black skirt. She was leaning against the jukebox with one hand, the other holding a beer bottle, trying to decide what record to play. While she sipped from the beer bottle, someone yelled, "Do a little dance, Paula."

Smiling as she turned to the man, she offered to strip if each gave her a dollar. She and the others looked at Dad in silence for several moments, as did I, curious about what he was going to say. He grinned, saying he'd give a dollar, then walked from behind the bar, closed the front door, pulled down the shade, and closed the shutters on the big windows. She collected twenty-three dollars, and in 1954, that was a good sum of money. After she put the money in her purse and handed it to my Dad for safekeeping, she dropped a nickel into the slot and pushed a button. As the song started, she danced around the floor, slowly unbuttoning her white blouse.

I was fifteen that summer, and like most kids of that era, I had never seen a naked woman. The closest I ever came to seeing one in those days were the models wearing underwear in a Montgomery Ward or Sears Catalog. Thinking it was a good idea for me to leave, I stood from the chair I was sitting on and gathered up my ink, pen, and paper.

As I walked past the end of the bar, Dad raised his hand and told me to sit down. "I want you to see this," he said with a big smile.

Feeling my face flush, I moved to an empty booth near the door to the kitchen and men's room, which was about as far away as I could get without leaving. I'm sure I stared at Paula with my mouth hanging open as she slowly pushed the unbuttoned white blouse over her shoulders, letting it fall to the floor, followed by her white bra. I couldn't help but stare at her small breasts as she started on the zipper of her black skirt. Smiling at me, she slowly pulled it down to the beat of the music, letting it drop to the floor, followed by her white panties. Stepping out of them, she danced her way around the jukebox and across the floor to the booth I was sitting in and slid into my seat.

She put her arms around me and kissed me on the cheek as my head filled with the smell of her perfume, feeling her warm body through my t-shirt. I looked at Dad standing behind the bar grinning at me. She stood, ruffled my hair with one hand, then danced around the other tables wearing only her black, flat shoes. I thought she was beautiful and could not take my eyes off of her, and by now, leaving had completely left my mind. In truth, I was glad Dad told me to stay, and I often wondered what Mary would have done had she walked in the back door that day.

As that memory left me, I turned from the jukebox to a half-filled saltshaker sitting on the dusty bar remembering the night James Monie, his friend Carl and I were sitting at the bar. I was sipping on a bottle of soda eating peanuts from a bag while listening to the two laughing as they drank beer and told funny stories of when they were in the army during the big war.

A man I had never seen before approached James and stood behind his stool. James Monie was a big man with dark, red curly hair who had been a paratrooper in WWII. James turned and asked if he could help him. The man looked drunk, had a mean look about him, and was unsteady on his feet as he leaned toward James and said something I could not hear. The smile left James' face, and suddenly he threw a left jab hitting the man in the face knocking him backward into the jukebox. As the needle raced across the 45rpm record, James knocked me off my stool as he grabbed a saltshaker from the bar. Getting the man in a headlock, he pounded him on the head with the saltshaker. The fight was over in a matter of seconds, with the man lying on the white and black spotted tile floor, face and head bleeding.

Dad suddenly appeared from behind the bar holding the small bat yelling for them to take it outside as he helped me up from the floor. James and Carl helped the poor soul outside, across the parking lot, sitting him down next to the front door of the bar next door. They were laughing when they returned, and as my Dad poured two glasses of cold beer, James put his hand on my shoulder, apologizing for knocking me off of the stool. After asking if I was alright, he told Dad to give me another soda.

Over the years, during my summer visits, I witnessed the occasional fistfight, such as a knifing that was not serious and a shooting in which no one got hurt. I became friends with addicts, pushers, and prostitutes who made the area around Washington Avenue and The Lone Texan their home. It was not uncommon to see a Houston Police Patrol Car slowly drive through the parking lot at night. It would occasionally stop for a few minutes while the officers sat in the car, looked in the two windows, and then drove out of the parking lot, disappearing up one of the side streets.

A prostitute named Darcy came to mind as I sat there. She was a woman in her late twenties or early thirties, and though she was pretty, she looked hard and older than her years. She spent a lot of time in the bar sipping a beer while waiting for a customer. I learned from Dad that she helped her younger brother Don with his heroin habit. During lean times she often pawned her watch or cheap jewelry with Dad for a few dollars, and he would hold them for her until she made enough money to buy them back. I thought she was nice, and at times she would sit at the table with me under the watchful eye of Dad and look at my drawings while we talked. Dad cautioned me on several occasions not to get too friendly with her, her brother, and some of the others. I guess he tried to protect me, but hell, I was already in the midst of the storm, so to speak.

The South was still the South in the fifties, and people of color were not allowed in bars, restaurants, bathrooms, or most other places white people gathered. Occasionally, on hot afternoons or warm evenings, a Negro man or two would come to the front door and raise a hand, holding up one or more fingers. Dad would get the beer from one of the coolers under the bar, take it to them, and collect their money. That made me think of the day Dad wanted Curley to drive him downtown in Dad's pickup. I don't recall why he wanted to go to the courthouse, but he had been drinking and was in a mood, so I decided to stay home. They came upon a demonstration by blacks that day near the courthouse. While stopping at a stop sign at the corner, a group of blacks suddenly surrounded the pickup. Police were trying to push the crowd back when a black man jumped on the running board of the passenger side of Dad's pickup, grabbed him by the shirt collar then called him a blue-eyed devil. Dad had already opened the glove compartment and was holding his thirty-eight snub-nose pistol and shot the man in the chest. As the man fell backward to the street, the crowd scattered. Dad was arrested, but a few days later, he was released, and the shooting was ruled justified and in self-defense.

Four

As that memory left me, my eyes found the booth where I sat one evening talking to a Houston Police Detective investigating the shooting of my Uncle Henry, my Dad's brother. I remembered he was a big man filling most of the booth as he sat across me. Beads of sweat formed across his forehead that he would occasionally wipe away with a crumpled, white hanky. He wore his thick head of gray hair in a crew cut, and the light blue suit he wore was wrinkled. He had taken off his suit coat before he sat down, and his white shirt was wet at the armpits and down the back.

While I talked about the events of the shooting of Uncle Henry, the stub of a pencil he held between the fat fingers of his big hand wrote down every word. I remember thinking how small the stub of pencil and notepad looked in his big hands. Occasionally he held up the hand holding the pencil, telling me to stop talking, then I watched in silence while he took a drink of cold beer. Setting the glass down, he told me to continue telling him what had happened.

The shooting of Uncle Henry

As best I recall, Dad had been visiting his brother Henry Greene when an argument broke out between Dad and Uncle Henry's son or stepson; I don't recall which. For the sake of the story, I will refer to him as the stepson. I never fully understood what the argument was over. At the time, I was sitting on the patio at Mary's drinking cold lemonade while listening to Evelyn read aloud from a book that didn't interest me.

Dad was upset all the next day about the argument, and later that night, he decided to drive to Henry's stepson's small farm west of Houston to clear the air. Mary happened to be in the bar that night and decided to ride along. I asked if I could go, Dad said okay, and then Curley, a friend of Dad's sitting at the end of the bar, asked if he could also come. Curley was thin, tall, dark-skinned with brown bloodshot eyes and thick black curly hair. He always looked hungover, and I suppose he was most of the time. Dad would pay him a few dollars when they would work on one of Mary's houses, or Curley would run errands for Dad to earn a couple of dollars or free beer.

After Dad told the barmaid, whose name was Frances, he would be back later, he, Mary, and Curley got in the cab of Dad's dark green 1949 Chevy pickup, each carrying a can of beer. I climbed into the pickup bed and sat down in the right front corner behind the cab. Once we were on the dark Hempstead Highway heading out of town, I stood and leaned against the cab feeling the warm night air rush past me. I looked up at the stars in the black, moonless night sky as laughter from inside the cab mixed with the hum of the engine and the tires on the paved highway. In the distance, I could see a movie playing on the screen of the Hempstead Drive-In theatre.

Minutes passed, and as I watched the headlights on the pavement ahead of us, the pickup slowed and turned off the highway onto a bumpy, dirt road. A scattering of lights from houses in the distance imitated stars in a black night sky as Dad drove along the lonely gravel road chasing the headlights. The pickup slowed, then Dad turned through the opening of a barbed-wire fence onto a narrow, rutted driveway. I could see Uncle Henry, his wife, stepson, and his family sitting in straight-back chairs in the yard under the glow of three floodlights.

Dad stopped, turned the engine off, the headlights, and stepped out of the truck's cab, standing behind the pickup door. Leaning with his elbows on the doors open window, he said hello. Uncle Henry offered Dad and the others a beer, but Dad thanked him, saying they brought their own from the bar. Dad and the stepson were talking, and Dad must have said something that set off Henry's stepson. Mary blurted something from inside the cab that angered the man who told Mary to shut up or he would shut her up. That just made things worse, and Dad said, "You do, you son-of-a-bitch, and I'll shoot your ass." Though that was an empty threat because Dad did not have a gun with him at the time, it was the wrong thing to say.

At that, the stepson set his bottle of beer down, jumped up from the chair he was sitting in, and ran to his pickup truck a few feet away. Taking a sixteen gauge pump shotgun from the gun rack inside the cab, he started walking toward Dad while yelling for him to go ahead and try and shoot him. Uncle Henry stood from his chair and told his stepson to put the gun away. Dad climbed back into the truck, and for some reason, I jumped from the back of the truck to the passenger side. Standing in the dark a few feet from the truck in the tall weeds filled with fear, I remember looking through the open window of the cab door past Curley and Mary at Dad's window.

Henry's stepson lifted the shotgun, pointed it at my Dad, and yelled something. The women yelled at the children to go inside as Uncle Henry hurried across the yard, yelling at his stepson to put the damn gun down. Mary tossed the can of beer she held out the window hitting the stepson in the face. Uncle Henry grabbed the shotgun by the barrel, and the two men struggled. I heard

Dad's truck start and the sound of grinding gears as he put it in reverse and backed out of the driveway. Suddenly the gun went off, and Uncle Henry fell backward, screaming in pain from being shot in the groin.

Terrified, I stood frozen in place while the warm night air filled with women screaming, children crying out, and Uncle Henry screaming in pain. His stepson dropped the gun, picked up Uncle Henry, carried him to his pickup, and placed him in the passenger side of the cab. Closing the door, he ran around to the driver's side, climbed in, and drove across the plowed furrows of the dark field with red taillights and headlights bouncing as it raced toward the highway.

Turning away from the lights of the pickup, I watched in horror as my aunt picked up the shotgun with the barrel pointing at her stomach. I wanted to warn her, but nothing came out of my mouth. Crying and cursing the gun, she pounded the wooden stock on the ground, trying to break it. Unable to do so, she tossed it into the weeds and then fell to her knees, looking up into the black night sky screaming at God. It was then that I heard Dad and Mary's voices calling me. Taking a last look at the scene, I ran down the long, dirt driveway as fast as my young legs would carry me. As I jumped into the back of the pickup, a neighbor's voice from the house across the dirt road yelled that she had called the police. Dad stepped on the gas spinning the wheels throwing dirt and gravel as the back of the truck swerved from side to side. As we headed for the Hempstead Highway at the end of the dirt road, I huddled in the corner next to the cab watching the floodlights fade into the darkness hoping Uncle Henry would be okay.

The next morning, Dad called the hospital to see how his brother, Henry, was, but they would not give any information over the telephone. He fretted most of the day about going to the hospital but felt it would be best if he stayed away, so he asked Mary to drive me to the hospital.

Once there, she waited outside on a cement bench by the steps while I went inside. As I approached the lady behind the information counter, I saw my Aunt Bill (real name Willamae), who had made the trip from San Antonio. Calling to her, she turned with a worried, sad face as I asked how Uncle Henry was. She said they had operated on him and that he was doing better than expected, and then she asked where my Dad was. I told her that he thought it would be best if he did not come to the hospital and sent me to see how his brother was. Her face and eyes filled with anger. "Tell my brother that he is not welcome here or anywhere else. Because of him, our brother may never walk again." Then she turned and disappeared up the crowded stairs, and that was the last time we ever spoke. Watching her walk up the stairs, I remember thinking how unfair that was to Dad when it was Henry's stepson that grabbed the shotgun in anger and would have killed Dad had it not been for Mary and Uncle Henry.

When Mary and I walked into The Lone Texan, Dad was standing behind the bar, drinking a beer and talking to Curley. He turned with hope in his eyes, and after I told him what his older sister had said, he just walked out of the bar. I started to follow, but Mary grabbed my arm and said to let him be. We watched as he walked across the parking lot, turned, and disappeared down Washington Avenue. She told Frances to look after things, then gently shoved me toward the door and the parking where her black Lincoln waited.

I spent the next several hours at Mary's while Evelyn tried to cheer me up, but I was worried about Dad and wanted to return to the bar. The hours had slowly passed when I told Mary that I was going to walk back to the bar. It was about a three-mile walk, but I wanted to be alone, and after protests from Mary, I left.

Walking into the Lone Texan Bar later that evening, Dad was drinking beer and playing shuffleboard for money with two other men. He turned and looked at me with his piercing blue eyes, and I knew he was in a foul mood and perhaps losing money at the game. Knowing how ugly he could get when drinking, I walked through the bar, out the back door, and into the house. After turning the radio to a rock and roll music station, I turned the fan on and lay down in the dark on the bed next to the open window. Looking at the screen door and rear of the building, bathed in light from the floodlights, I wished I could go home.

A few days later, the shooting of Uncle Henry was judged accidental, and Dad and I never spoke of that night or Uncle Henry again.

Five

While that memory faded, my eyes made their journey around the dim, quiet room as my mind filled with the faces of people sitting at the bar or in booths drinking beer, laughing, and having a good time. My eyes settled on an eight by ten black and white photograph of me when I was in the Navy, wearing my dungaree shirt and sporting the beginnings of a beard. Dad had tacked the photo to the wall behind the bar under one of the many small, now dead, neon signs advertising beer. I had forgotten that I had sent it to him while in the Navy, and it made me feel good that he had placed it behind the bar for others to see.

Sitting in the silence of the small world my father once ruled over that was now gone forever, I couldn't help but feel sorry for him. You could not excuse him as an alcoholic because he was not an alcoholic; he just liked to drink. The problem was that when he drank, he got mean. His temper was hot and quick, and my back and bottom felt the sting of his belt many times, as did my three older brothers until they got too big. Thinking back, I believe my mother lived in fear for most of her life.

Hearing a noise, I turned and saw him walking through the doorway from the kitchen into the bar area. He glanced around the silent room in memory as he pulled the stool next to mine from under the bar and dusted it off with one hand. His blue eyes lit up, and a small smile filled his puffy face as he softly said, "This old place has sure seen better days." Sitting down, he softly chuckled as he talked about times past and those that walked in and out of The Lone Texan Bar.

I asked about Paula, and he said that someone found her in the park just a few blocks from Washington Avenue dead from an overdose a few years back. Sadness filled his face when I asked about James Monie. He told me that he died last year from a heart attack and there were a lot of people at his funeral. I learned that Darcy was dead, Dad didn't know from what, and her brother Don was in prison for armed robbery. I asked about the old man who would shuffle in, sit at the bar, and leave with either Darcy or Paula after a half glass of beer.

"That was old man, Monie," he said with laughter.

Surprised, I asked if that was James Monie's father. Dad laughed and said it was. I never knew the old man's name as he shuffled in and out of the bar with small, quick steps. As Dad and I talked about others that I had come to know, Dad said that most were gone, but occasionally he would see someone walking along Washington Ave. I asked about Curley and learned that he was still around the neighborhood. Though curious, I never asked about Uncle Henry, and Dad never brought it up.

The big, white-faced clock above the door to the men's room; the only thing still working in this quiet, lifeless room, said it was time to leave. Not knowing when or if I would be back, I took a long look around the empty, dusty room as memories I had long ago forgotten traveled through my mind. Saying it was time to go, I stood, pushed my stool back under the bar, and followed Dad around the corner of the bar, through the kitchen, and out the back door. While he locked up, I went into the house and retrieved my bag that I had left by the door earlier that morning. Stepping outside with it, I made sure the door was locked, quietly closed the screen door, and followed the narrow sidewalk to the gate in the chain-link fence where Dad waited.

While I waited by the car for Dad to lock the gate, a tall, skinny man rounded the corner of the parking lot dressed in a wrinkled, white, long-sleeved shirt and wrinkled, dirty, tan pants. As he walked across the parking lot towards us, I recognized it was Curley. Once a relatively good-looking man, his thick head of black, curly hair was a little thinner, filled with gray, and in need of a haircut. His brown eyes were bloodshot as they always were, and some of his teeth were missing. His tanned, lined face needed a shave, and he looked older, thinner, and fragile, unlike the man I remembered. I quickly recalled the night Uncle Henry was shot and other times when Dad would drink too much and mistreat the man. But something between them allowed their friendship to endure, and he never left Dad's side. We exchanged hellos and how are you, and as we shook hands, Dad asked him if he wanted to ride along to the bus terminal. He said he would, so I climbed in the back of the Mercury with my bag while Curley sat upfront.

As the car pulled away from the bar, I turned in the seat and stared through the rear window at the lifeless white building until we turned out of the parking lot onto Washington Ave. After it disappeared behind another building, my eyes found the big sign, The Lone Texan Bar sitting atop a steel pole at the edge of the parking lot next to the street. I turned from the sign and listened as Curley told Dad a joke that was not all that funny, but Dad laughed anyway. Looking out the open window at the buildings passing by and feeling the hot Texas air on my skin, I was anxious to return to Denver and a cooler climate. Suddenly and without warning, the sadness of leaving found me as my eyes settled on the side of my Dad's face as he drove along Washington Avenue, and I knew I would miss him.

Pulling into a parking spot next to the curb across the street from the Greyhound Bus Terminal, Dad put the car in park, turned off the ignition, then turned in his seat, resting his arm on the back of the front seat. He looked at me with sad, blue eyes saying he was glad I made the trip. I said I was too, shook Curley's hand, then took Dad's hand in mine, feeling him squeeze it as we shook hands for a long moment. Letting go, I grabbed my bag and opened the car door, and as I turned and looked into Dad's red eyes, I thought he was about to cry, which surprised me. I said goodbye, quickly climbed out, and before I closed the door, he told me to be careful and asked me to write. Smiling, I said I would, and would call him in a couple of weeks, then I closed the door and stepped back onto the sidewalk. Dad started the car, and as he drove away from the curb, Curley leaned out the window and yelled, "Take care, Richard," then he smiled a toothless grin as he waved goodbye.

Standing on the sidewalk, I watched that 1953 blue Mercury as memories of a younger father I loved and idolized as a young boy. As the car turned and disappeared around the next corner, emotions I never expected came over me. I wiped my eyes and then looked both ways before crossing the busy street toward the depot. Stepping onto the sidewalk of the bus terminal, I paused at the door for a last look up the street empty street, imagining Dad driving the car and talking to Curley. As my mind pushed the bad times away, it filled with good memories of Dad, and a smile filled my face. Opening the door of the bus depot, I stepped inside.

I suppose I made my peace with Dad that trip, and although I loved him and thought of him often, the years and life got in the way as they often do. The letter I promised never left my mind, nor the phone call made. My father, Edward Lee Greene, was alone when he passed away from an aneurysm in the dark, early morning hours of April 25, 1974. He was 67. His way of life had taken its toll on his once firm, strong body, making him older than his years. He lived his life the way he wanted while the rest of us wished it had been different. When I think of him today, I try and think of happy times and not those when I feared him. My Dad was two people. One sober and good, a man you could not help but like with a laugh that brought laughter. The other was a mean, angry drunk with piercing blue eyes and a quick temper.

Years after the divorce, my mother met a nice, easy-going man she married and had a very good life until she passed away at 98. My brother Jerry passed away from Cancer in 1984. Edward Lee Greene Jr. contracted aides from a blood transfusion after a motorcycle accident in 1988. My brother Malcolm passed away on February 21, 2020, from Leukemia, leaving me the last of the family.

I never returned to Houston, not even for Dad's funeral. It was too late. That final day in Houston, as he sat in the

Mercury with red eyes, was the last time I saw or spoke to my Dad. Not hugging him that day when we said goodbye is something I have regretted since his passing. I never saw or spoke to Mary, Elizabeth, or Evelyn again, and I can only guess what became of Curley after Dad passed away. Now, in the twilight years of my own life, I have realized too late that life and time do not offer second chances.

Other books by Richard Greene

Death of Innocence

The book Death of Innocence is a story about five families of my ancestors who lived during the Civil War. The story is based on fact, along with fiction and family lore. What happened to each of these families, for the most part, is true, but I also added some fiction to fill in the gaps. Joseph Samuel Greene, the main character, was my great-grandfather. I think you will find the story interesting as well as entertaining.

Befriended by a slave and the captain of a riverboat, a young runaway named Joseph Samuel Greene finds adventure on the river and the love of a young Mary McAlexander. The Civil War will not only test their love for one another, but the faith of the McAlexander, Chrisman, and Patterson families as each endures the war's death and destruction.

Death rides across the South in the guise of the southern home guard, taking the innocent without hesitation, or regret. The sorrow they leave will last forever as each proud family endures while losing their innocence.

Wade Garrison's Promise

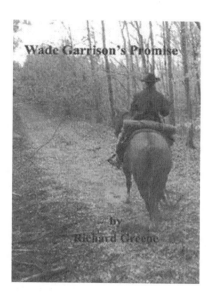

Wade Garrison is a simple man who, as a young man, came west chasing the stories he had read about in cheap western novels while growing up on a farm in South Carolina. He is not a violent man, and like most men of humble beginnings, he holds his name and promises in high regard.

Watching the pine coffin containing his friend, Emmett Spears's, lifeless body lowered into the dark grave, Wade makes a silent promise of revenge. It is a promise that will take him far from the girl he loves and the Circle T Ranch in eastern Colorado.

As young Wade Garrison trails the four men responsible for his friend's death, he will soon find himself unprepared for the death and violence he will find. He is unaware that in fulfilling his promise to avenge Emmett Spears, he will lose himself in the process.

God's Coffin

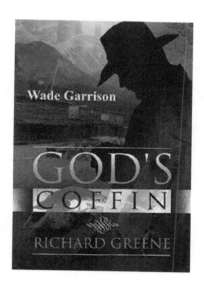

Sequel to Wade Garrison's Promise

Wade Garrison rides out of Harper, Colorado, into the New Mexico Territory in 1872, believing he is riding away from a troubled past.

Now, six years later, his old friend, Sheriff Seth Bowlen, in Sisters, Colorado, is in trouble and needs help. Sheriff Bowlen sends a wire to United States Marshal Billy French in Santa Fe, who, in turn, sends Deputy Marshal Wade Garrison to help their old friend.

Innocently, Wade decides to take his wife Sarah, and son Emmett, with him so they can visit her family in Harper, a small town northeast of Sisters. As he and his family board the train in Santa Fe, he could not have known that a terrible storm of violence was already brewing, and this fateful decision could destroy his wife and child.

Atonement

Sequel to God's Coffin

In August 1878, Wade Garrison took his vengeance against the men who took the life of his unborn daughter and tried to kill his wife and son to settle a score. When the last man was dead from Wade's Sharps Rifle, he rode out of Harper, Colorado, a wanted man, and disappeared into the Montana Territory.

Morgan Hunter was a forty-eight-year-old gunman from west Texas wanted for shooting and killing a sheriff and his deputy. Fleeing from those killings and riding away from the sorrow that caused them, he rode into the Montana Territory. Unaware of the other, both men rode toward the same destiny.

Sarah looked toward the top of the hill every day, waiting for Wade and his red sorrel mare to come home. The days turned into weeks, and then into months, and still no word of him or from him.

Wade Garrison

The Last Ride

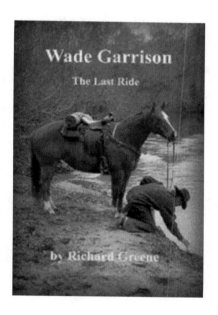

Sequel to Atonement

It has been a year since Wade was shot and nearly died after being found innocent of murder at his trial in Harper, Colorado. Keeping his promise to God and Sarah, his Colt pistol lies tucked away in the bottom drawer of a chest in his bedroom, and the Sharps rifle covered in the rawhide sheath stands in a corner behind the chest. While he misses the life of a United States Deputy Marshal, he is content being with his wife Sarah, son Emmett, and daughter Mary Louise on their ranch.

Unknown to Wade and Sarah, he is about to be thrust into a life of violence once again by events that take place in the small town of Harper, Colorado. When the people of Harper seek his help for justice, the old life pulls at him. Resisting those old ways, he fears the town, and his son will think he is a coward. How can he break his promises not only to Sarah but to God?

Feeding the Beast

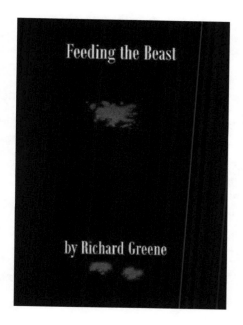

1951

It is 1951 in Denver, Colorado, and the investigation into the murders of young teenage girls by Denver Homicide Detective Dan Morgan brings back suppressed memories of the murder of his identical twin brother thirty-one years ago. He and his partner, Jack Brolin, are getting nowhere in their investigation when the killer calls Morgan at Police

47

Headquarters. With the help of a psychologist, Dan slowly begins to understand why the killer calls him, and what he wants from him.

The Second World War has been over for six years, and the United States is now involved militarily in Korea, termed a Police Action rather than a war. On April 10, President Harry S. Truman fires General Douglas MacArthur, commander of the United States forces in Korea. This action resulted in the president's lowest approval rating of 23%, which remains the lowest of any serving president.

The Denver Police Department protecting a population of fewer than 415,000 residents was small compared to cities such as Chicago, New York, and Los Angeles.

The use of DNA by the judicial system is far in the future, electrically powered streetcars were the primary source of transportation, and soon to be replaced by electric buses. Computers were in their infancy, and while most old newspapers and other public records are on microfilm, thousands of documents are not. Not every home could afford a television, so the radio remained the household's nightly entertainment. The closest thing to a cellular telephone was Dick Tracy's two-way wristwatch found in the comics, so the police had to rely on rotary telephones and shortwave radios. Being Mirandized was not an option criminals were given in 1951, and would not be until 1966.

The term 'Serial Killer' would not be coined until 1970 by FBI Special Agent Robert Reesler.

Made in the USA
Middletown, DE
26 August 2024

59255223R00033